The Cat in the Hat's Learning Library

The editors would like to thank
BARBARA KIEFER, Ph.D., Associate Professor of Reading and Literature,
Teachers College, Columbia University, and
PAUL L. SIESWERDA, Aquarium Curator,
Aquarium for Wildlife Conservation, New York,
for their assistance in the preparation of this book.

---

www.randomhouse.com/seussville

Library of Congress Cataloging-in-Publication Data
Worth, Bonnie.
Wish for a fish : all about sea creatures / by Bonnie Worth ; illustrated by Aristides Ruiz.
    p.   cm. — (The Cat in the Hat's learning library)   Includes index.
SUMMARY: In rhyming text, the Cat in the Hat introduces Sally and Dick to the various
inhabitants of the ocean, including herring, mackerel, jellyfish, sharks, manatees, and whales.
ISBN 0-679-89116-1 (trade). — ISBN 0-679-99116-6 (lib. bdg.)
1. Marine animals—Juvenile literature.   [1. Marine animals.]   I. Ruiz, Aristides, ill.   II. Title.
III. Series: Cat in the Hat's learning library.   QL122.2.W685   1999   591.77—dc21   98-34709

Printed in the United States of America   10 9 8 7 6

WISH FOR A FISH

by Bonnie Worth

illustrated by

Aristides Ruiz

The Cat in the Hat's Learning Library™

Random House 🏠 New York

I'm the Cat in the Hat,
and I hear that you wish
to go down to the sea
and to visit the fish.

So please climb on board
S.S. Undersea Glubber.
It is made out of shark skin
and very fine rubber.

It will take us down deep—
deep down under the sea.
We will start at the top
and go deep as can be.

The top parts are sunny.
The bottom parts black.
We'll go to the bottom
and then we'll come back.

Sunny Zone,

Twilight Zone,

Dark Zone,

Abyss—

the Trench at the bottom
you won't want to miss!

Sunny Zone—sea level to 660 feet

The Sunny Zone is
where our sea visit starts.
Most of our sea life
is found in these parts.

The law of the sea
is the same as on land.
I'll call it the food chain
so you'll understand.

Big fish eat smaller fish
and so on until...
you get down to
one of the tiniest—
krill.

11

If you're wishing for fish,
there are lots of them here.
I see herring and mackerel
swimming quite near.

THING 1

MACKEREL

HERRING

SUNNY

PERCH

COD

CATFISH

Fish can lay eggs.
They have fins and fish tails.
And most fish have bodies
all covered with scales.
These scales, they are coated
with slippery slime.
The slime keeps out germs—
at least, most of the time.

13

Fish open their mouths
and they let water in.
That's when the gills' job
really starts to kick in.

Gills sift through the water
and pull out the "air."*
They help the fish find
all the "air" that is there.

(*Oxygen, really.)

AURELIA

COMPASS

The jellyfish is
a most interesting fella.
He looks kind of like
a transparent umbrella!

SUNNY ZONE

COMB JELLY

Stay away from his tentacles
(those long stringy things).
They stun prey by giving off
hundreds of stings!

CYANEA

Of the hundreds of kinds
of sharks in the sea,
we only have time now
to visit with three.

The six-inch-long dogfish
(no, it never barks),

the fifty-foot whale shark

(the Mack truck of sharks)—

and what have we here?

19

It is called the great white
for its white belly, great teeth,
and great big deep bite!
A shark grows its teeth
in neat rows in its face.
When the front row wears out,
the next row takes its place.

Shark bodies are made
of the same kind of stuff

SUNNY ZONE

as your ears and your nose—
that's what makes them so tough.
The stuff is called cartilage.
It folds and it bends.
And when it is torn,
the cartilage mends.

21

What else can we see
in this nice sunny water?

Oh, say, see the manatee
and her calf daughter!

SUNNY ZONE

Manatees are mammals
like you and like me.
They have lungs
and give milk
to their babies, you see.

Another sea mammal
we'll see is the whale.
It's the largest of mammals
we'll see, without fail.
The great whale family
is split into two:
toothed whales
(like the orca)
and baleen
(like the blue).

TOOTHED

BALEEN

Baleen fills the blue whale's
mouth like a grill.
As water flows through it,
it strains out the krill.

SUNNY ZONE

The blue whale weighs tons,
maybe ninety or more.
It's bigger than even
a big dinosaur!

These toothed whales are orcas,
and few can defeat them.
They like to hunt seals
and to catch them and eat them!

NARWHAL

The narwhal's one tusk
sticks out like a horn.
It looks so much like
a one-horned unicorn!

All whales hold their breath
when they dive down below,
and when they come up,
let it out with a blow!

RIGHT WHALE

27

Before we go deeper,
let's all wave hello
to our mammal pals, dolphins—
that's them down below.

A dolphin can see
in the night—wonder why?
Echolocation.
It works like an eye.
It sends out a click
and the click bounces back.
And the sound of that click
helps the dolphin keep track
of where it is going
and which fish is where
and whether some foe,
like a shark, might be there.

Shake hands with the octopus.
Isn't it great?
With arm after arm just
for hugging. Yikes—eight!
Dear Dick and sweet Sally,
tell me, what would you think
if I told you the octopus
shoots out a dark ink?

It squirts out the ink
in some enemy's face
and then swims away
to a much safer place.

SUNNY ZONE

29

Twilight Zone—660 to 3,300 feet

Of all of the fights
that are fought in the sea,
there's one that is biggest,
if you're asking me.

Do I hear you asking?
(I'm so glad you did!)
It's sperm whale
versus giant squid!

Like all whales, the sperm
whale must come up for air.
But this one can dive
and then stay way down there
for two hours or more—
at three thousand feet—
shopping for giant
squid to eat.

Dark Zone—3,300 to 13,200 feet

Get out your flashlights.
It's dark way down here!
And the fish are beginning
to look very queer!

The gigantura and
the big-mouth eel.

The whipnose,
which comes with its own
rod and reel.

FLASHLIGHT
FISH

Down here it is always
as black as the night,
so many fish here have
their very own light.
They use it to locate
a mate or some prey.
Food-hunting is hard
like this, day after day.

Abyss—13,200 to 19,800 feet

You won't find many
creatures in this deep, cold sea.

Sea cucumber, sea spider,
and tripod are three.

The Abyss has a carpet
of thick, yucky muck.
Animals have legs so
they will not get stuck.

Trench—19,800 feet and deeper

Before we go up,
it is really a must
that you visit the vents, which
are cracks in Earth's crust.

It is up through these vents
that the hot waters spout
and warm up these clams
and these worms here about.

Giant clams and tube worms
have enough things to eat
because this deep spot
has unusual heat.

Oh, say, can you see
by my undersea clock—
it is time the fair Glubber
got back to the dock.

And now that our trip
below sea is all done,
I will bet that you two
have a wish for some...

GLOSSARY

Abyss: A hole almost too deep to measure.

Defeat: To beat in a contest.

Foe: Enemy.

Locate: To find.

Lungs: The two sac-like organs mammals use for breathing.

Oxygen: A gas that is found in air. Oxygen is also found in water and in rock. Animals need oxygen to live.

Prey: An animal hunted for food.

Stun: To shock or cause a person or animal to lose its senses.

Transparent: Something so light that you can see through it.

Trench: A deep ditch.

Tusk: A very long animal tooth.

Versus: Against—a word used to describe two people or animals that are engaged in a contest.

FOR FURTHER READING

Amazing Fish by Mary Ling, photographed by Jerry Young (Alfred A. Knopf, *Eyewitness Juniors*). Closeup photos of exotic fish. For grades 1 and up.

Dolphins by Bob Talbot (Little Simon, *The Cousteau Society*). Closeup photos depict dolphins swimming, playing, and leaping gracefully through the air. For preschoolers and up.

Sea Animals by Angela Royston, illustrated by Jane Cradock-Watson and Dave Hopkins; photographed by Steve Shott (Little Simon, *Eye Openers*). Photos and illustrations of the most fascinating creatures in the sea. For preschoolers and up.

The Seashore by Gallimard Jeunesse and Elisabeth Cohat, illustrated by Pierre de Hugo (Scholastic, *A First Discovery Book*). A look at the place where the sea meets the land. For preschoolers and up.

Whales and Other Creatures of the Sea by Joyce Milton, illustrated by Jim Deal (Random House, *Picturebacks*®). All about whales and other creatures who roam the oceans. For preschoolers and up.

INDEX